TEN HOUSES

TEN HOUSES

Edited by Oscar Riera Ojeda

Gwathmey Siegel

ROCKPORT
PUBLISHERS

Rockport Publishers, Inc.
Rockport, Massachusetts

First published in the United States of America by:

Rockport Publishers, Inc.

146 Granite Street

Rockport, Massachusetts 01966

Telephone: 508-546-9590

Fax: 508-546-7141

Distributed to the book trade and art trade in the U.S. by:

The AIA Press

1735 New York Avenue

Washington, DC 20006

Telephone: 800-365-ARCH

Fax: 800-678-7102

Other distribution by:

Rockport Publishers, Inc.

Rockport, Massachusetts 01966

ISBN   1-56496-216-4

10 9 8 7 6 5 4 3 2 1

Manufactured in Hong Kong by Regent Publishing Services Limited

Cover Photo/Page 2: Bechtler Residence, Photo by Richard Bryant/Arcaid

Graphic Design: Lucas H. Guerra / Oscar Riera Ojeda

Contents

Selected Works

Text by Megan Moynihan

Foreword

by Oscar Riera Ojeda

Over the course of three decades the firm of Gwathmey Siegel & Associates Architects has created a body of work of lasting significance and continuing impact. The design of houses brought Gwathmey Siegel their first international recognition, and led to the freedom to test their theories and principals on a larger scale. Not only has their residential work provided a laboratory for their own experiments in museum, educational, and corporate design, but its provocative ideas have exerted a strong influence on the work of both their peers and younger generations of architects. It is therefore appropriate that we have chosen them as the subject of the first volume in the series *Ten Houses*—a series that will look at recent developments in American architecture through the in-depth examination of the residential work of both well-established practitioners and younger architects.

To limit the number of projects in this book to ten may seem counterproductive given the abundance of work that Gwathmey Siegel has produce over the past thirty years. Many of the important and historically recognized homes that the architects designed in the 1960s and 1970s cannot be included in these pages. Ten houses are certainly too few if we wish to document the firm's methodology or explore the varied approaches to space and materials that have characterized their investigations.

Perhaps the most important challenge we face will be to portray the architectural character of each home without being able to physically explore the constructed space. Knowing this, we have compiled detailed representations of each project, with the desire to "open their doors" as widely as possible. These works, whose artistic value goes beyond mere construction and the solution to our most basic and mundane needs, have been chosen to express the clients' requirements and lifestyles through the architects' creative vision.

Introduction

by Charles Gwathmey

We believe that the house is central to the tradition of architecture. Civilization requires shelter, and history, both written and archeological, is inseparable from the history of houses. We also believe that it is hardly eccentric to conceive of houses as architecture, since our process both assumes and demonstrates the identity of the house as a formal conception of structure, as well as an organization of program in relation to spaces.

Our houses always have been test cases that address an entire range of architectural issues—history and context; site influences; arrival, procession, and circulation; scale and proportion; light; private versus public domains; and the technology of construction—which are prioritized by research and interpretative analysis as tools of exploration and design.

Our houses are formal investigations in which archetypes of general application, rather than incidental resources for habitation, are the objects of study. This does not mean that they are not programmatically responsive. However, each, in its own terms, examines the ideal composite overlay of site/sequence, plan/section, transparency/spatial layering, solid/void, and form/space to manifest the essence of the idea.

It is implicit in the concept of the house as a building created by an architectural process that the qualities and characteristics that are perceptually available are not merely expressions of a preconceived set of images. Similarly, the determining principles of this work are not specific to a formula of accommodation or the expression of personality, but arise from a less arbitrary analysis of requirements and possibilities. The forms have immediate relevance to the occupants, but the solutions are based upon an ordering and assembly process that engages both perception and speculation. It is a process of discovery and editing that generates essential composite relationships between object and site, program and form.

Over the years, we have developed a horizontal and vertical planning grid which incorporates Le Corbusier's Modulor. This interlocking system functions

not as a schematic arbiter of form, but as a practical design tool and geometric reference, investing departure from its order with a sense of meaningful variation and spatial intensity.

An important confrontation in our work relates to the line of interpretation and meaning between abstraction and representation. If there is a correlation with painting and sculpture, our work clearly refers to the Cubist approach of collage and assemblage, as opposed to the non-representational or the representational.

Our clients become patrons and are totally involved in this interactive discovery process. The intellectual goal is to approach each project as a new opportunity: to eliminate habit; avoid "taste" and never use the word "like"; and to develop a rational dialogue, the conclusion of which, after assumptions are tested, is the result of elimination and formal resolution.

We believe that research, to gain information and provoke the redefinition of alternatives, is positive. Research as confirmation is redundant. Eclecticism is not a process of discovery and risk; I suggest it is not a process that produces art. Architects create art not by reconstituting the known, but through invention and interrogation. These ten houses represent an ongoing investigation that, by circumstance and obligation, generates speculation as well as resolution.

Previous Spread: *(Top) Taft Residence. Cincinnati, Ohio; (Bottom Left) Weitz Residence. Quogue, New York; (Bottom Right) Haupt Residence. Amagansett, New York*
Opposite Page: *Gwathmey Residence and Studio. Amagansett, New York*

deMenil Residence

East Hampton, New York

Above: *The view across the dunes renders the manmade as an abstract "cornice" on the landscape.*

Opposite Page: *The brise-soleil is both a filter between the interior and the landscape, and a frame that is progressively eroded from the screened porch to the triple-height "gate" between site and ocean at the west.*

The challenge of the deMenil residence was to develop a group of buildings, including a guesthouse, garage, and caretaker's house, that responded both to the scale of the seven-acre dune site facing the Atlantic Ocean and the vernacular of the great beach houses of the Hamptons.

Designed in 1979, the house can be seen as the culmination of the formal investigations of the preceding decade, defining public and private realms through the manipulation of spatial volumes within a clearly articulated rectangular framework, and dissolving and redefining the boundaries between the interior and the landscape through the layering of building and site elements.

A stucco wall, running between the caretaker's house and the pond at the north end of the site, forms a gate that marks the beginning of an allée that leads to the ocean. Passing through a series of increasingly structured layers of landscape elements—pond, woods, tennis court, formal garden, trellis, and lawn—the driveway arrives at the autocourt, where a second stucco wall, edged by a reflecting pool, extends and completes the north facade of the house. The main building thus becomes both a destination and a second gate, intersected by the axis of the allée to form an indoor zone (house) and an outdoor zone (pool) of equal dimensions.

The house is developed in four layers parallel to the ocean. An eroded two-story entry space penetrates the first zone, in which a four-story greenhouse, framed within the facade, marks the transition between the landscape and the interior. Vertical cedar siding, used for both the exterior cladding and the interior wall and ceiling finishes, recalls the shingle houses of the twenties, and reinforces the interplay between interior and exterior space.

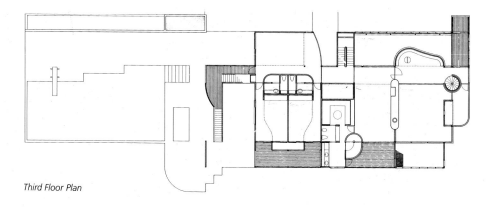

Third Floor Plan

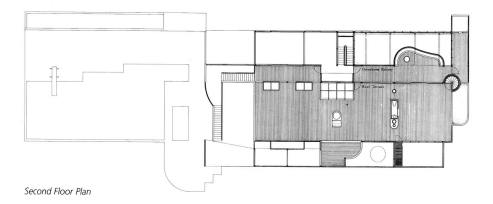

Second Floor Plan

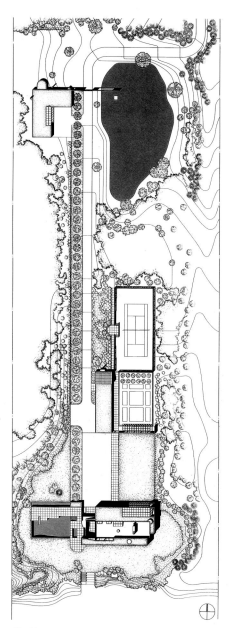

Site Plan

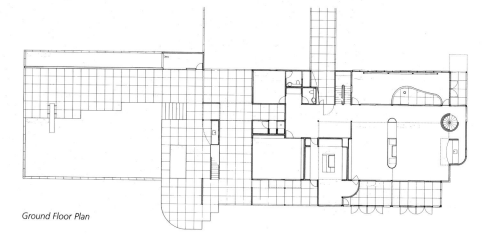

Ground Floor Plan

Left: A hanging stair in the triple-height screened porch connects the deck of the master bedroom to the roof terrace. The occulus in the brise-soleil establishes the roof plane as a facade and articulates the deck as a two-story space with its own "skylight."

Above: The wall adjacent to the pool terrace is one of several colored masonry stucco site walls (which include the entry gate, the guesthouse, and the fireplace wall) that act as markers in the landscape and establish site sequence and layering.

Right: The greenhouse roof opens and closes automatically to maintain a pre-set temperature range.

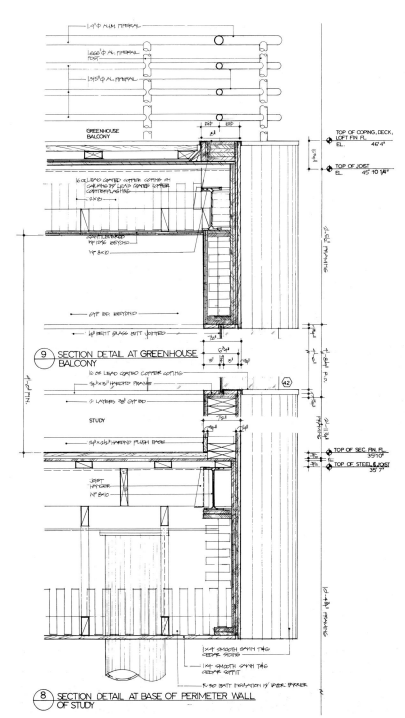

This Page: *The aluminum frame structures of the three-story greenhouse and screened porch are transparent spatial layers as well as "thick walls" that bracket the interior living spaces.*

The narrow second zone is given over to a three-story entrance hall and a circulation spine that runs the length of the building, leading west to the pool terrace. The third zone is occupied by the common living areas: den, kitchen and breakfast room, dining room, and double-height living room. The final zone is a brise-soleil, carved out of the southern facade, that accommodates a three-story screened porch and terrace, and mediates both visually and physically between the interior and the dunes.

On the second floor, elements within each zone begin to assert themselves as volumes in adjacent layers, and the boundaries between landscape and house are further subverted. The master bath pushes into the brise-soleil, creating a separation between the terraces of the guest and master bedrooms. The library flows into the zone of the greenhouse. In section, a series of double- and triple-height spaces interpenetrates the floors. The vertical circulation sequence culminates in the roof garden, an outdoor room that looks through the frame of the brise-soleil into the "indoor" triple-height screened porch and out towards the ocean.

The spine of the house extends back across the allée, then turns as it descends to the swimming pool terrace, forming an anteroom to both the pool and the beach, and integrating the primary north-south layering of the site with its secondary east-west layering. The allée continues out to the shoreline through the final monumental gate to the ocean, an extension of the brise-soleil which anchors the house and gives it a sense of scale and proportion relative to both the activities of the occupants and the broad expanse of the dunes.

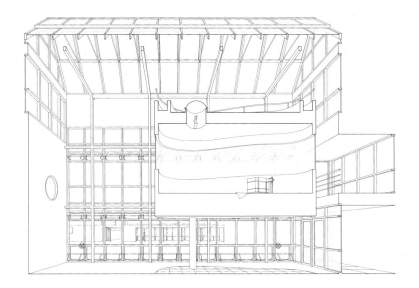

Garey Residence
Kent, Connecticut

Located on a four-acre woodland site with a natural stream along its northern boundary, the Garey residence marks the transition from the layered approach to spatial organization evident in the deMenil residence to one in which mass and volume exert their independence from the frame. The parti responds to the topography of the site by using the natural slope to create a transition between arrival in the autocourt and the private wilderness area beyond the house. The half-level circulation system that integrates the house into the landscape also addresses the owners' desire for privacy and a clear separation between parents' and children's sleeping spaces.

The L-shaped orthogonal frame of the house is divided into four zones: the garage, at ground level; the common living areas, a half-level above; the children's bedrooms, over the garage; and the master bedroom, another half-level up, overlooking the cut cylinder of the double-height living room. From the entry hall in the circulation tower where the two wings intersect, the stairs proceed by half-flights to each level, knitting the section of the building into the sloped terrain. The vertical circulation sequence culminates in a rooftop study opening to a deck overlooking the woods and hills to the north. An outdoor stair leads from the second floor landing of the children's wing down to the pool terrace, engaging the northern side of the house in an informal "courtyard" bordered by the existing stone wall.

The horizontal circulation sequence culminates in the two-and-a-half story glazed, cylindrical living room that looks out over a stream cascading across the northeastern edge of the site. A stucco hearth links it with the more intimate family room behind. Above, the mahogany-framed windows of the master bedroom curve around behind the chimney to create an oculus to the out-of-doors. Over the dining room, the cedar wall of the master bath slices the transparent volume of the cylinder, locking it into the orthogonal, cedar-clad frame of the house. The living room becomes both an object in a frame and an object in the woods, the place where interior and landscape merge.

Roof Level

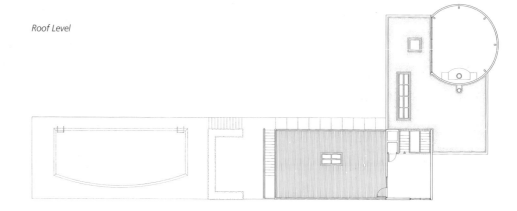

Second and Third Levels

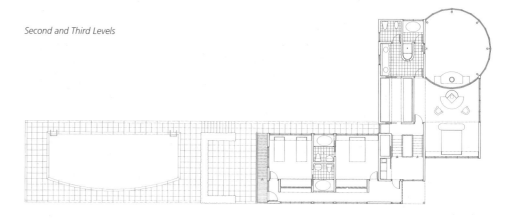

Ground and First Levels

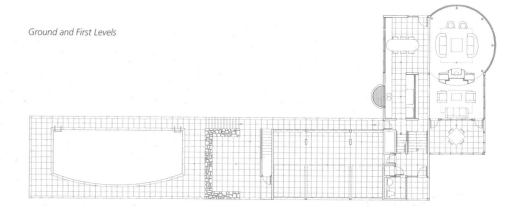

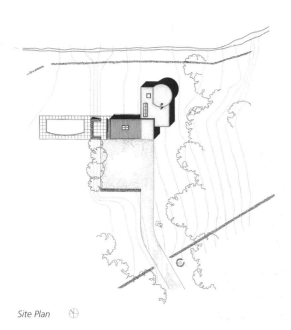

Site Plan

Left: *From the woods, the glazed cylinder of the living space reads as an extension of the stream, fragmenting light as it is reflected from the faceted planes of the windows.*
The west wing is articulated by windows that establish the planes of the orthogonal walls and mediate the transition from the cylinder to the frame of the house.

Right: *The pool terrace is a plan extension of the west wing that forms the edge of a court-yard created by the L-shape of the house and an existing stone wall to the north. The stone retaining wall defines an outdoor room and mediates the change in grade between the pool and the house.*

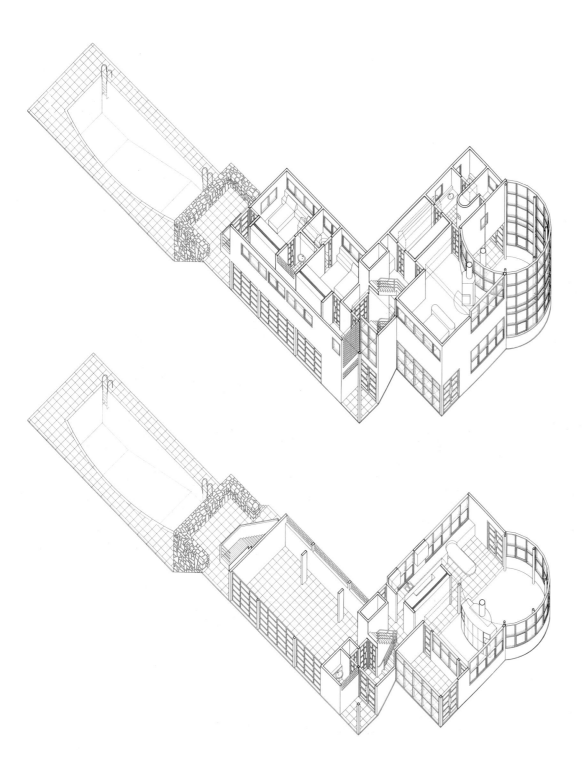

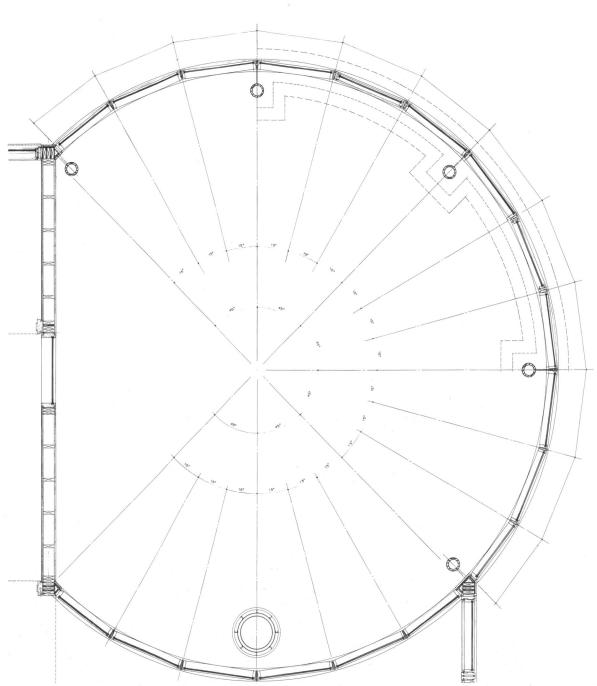

Opposite Page: *The wall of the master bathroom cuts through the quarter points of the cylinder, and five freestanding columns define a half-circle rotated on a forty-five degree angle from the orthogonal grid of the house to face the landscape. The curve of the cylinder extends past the centerline to form the wall of the bedroom, creating a geometry of closure rather than shear, and the implication of whole rather than segment.*

Right: The disengaged round columns provide vertical reinforcement for the window wall and add a structural inner layer that creates a second frame without compromising transparency. A single square column marks the corner of the volume carved from the house to accommodate the cylinder.

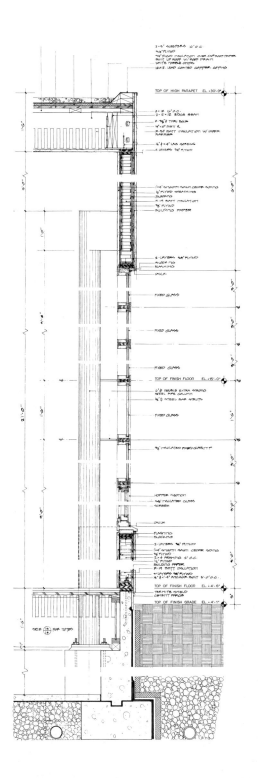

This Page: *The fireplace and chimney are treated as a free-standing object that mediates between the volume of the double-height living-room and the more private sitting area beyond. Cedar siding clads the interior walls and ceilings, reinforcing the ambiguity between indoor and outdoor spaces.*

Spielberg Residence

East Hampton, New York

The Spielberg residence is located on the edge of a saltwater pond on a six-acre field in East Hampton. The owners' desire for a house that would peacefully coexist with the landscape, and a home scaled for comfort and privacy, rather than to impress, harmonized with local restrictions on the development of the pond's shoreline. The challenge was to design a structure that would retain the texture and feeling of the old summer bungalows and converted farms of the area, without becoming an imitation "old house."

The eighteenth-century Pennsylvania Dutch barn that forms the underlying structure of the house provided an unorthodox solution to the dilemma, and led to a building that is unique in the firm's oeuvre. Dismantled and moved from a site that was slated to become an office park, the barn was approached not as a historical type to be preserved—that is, restored to its original condition—but as a "found object" to be transformed. The exterior becomes an abstract volume, punctured by deep-set wood frame windows and clad in cedar shingles that recall the vernacular architecture of the area without distorting the barn's iconic shape. The 52-foot by 52-foot frame and original oak siding are revealed inside, preserving two centuries of weathering in the ceiling and perimeter walls. Partitions between rooms are finished in a smooth plaster that creates an inverted half-timbered appearance while emphasizing the distinction between the original structure and the interventions.

Both architecture and landscape are revealed as a series of fragments, beginning with arrival in the autocourt, which affords a glimpse of the pond, and culminating in expansive views of the dunes and the ocean from the upstairs windows. A carriage house screens the main building from the autocourt and forms the gate to a pear-tree courtyard whose dimensions echo the footprint of the barn. The main axis of arrival leads to a shingled entrance porch; a cross-axial path leads west to the swimming pool terrace overlooking the pond.

Above: The clarity of the spatial hierarchy of the original barn frame both informed and resolved the parti.

Opposite Page: Seen from across the pond, the gatehouse, courtyard, and barn are sited as an assemblage that establishes a sense of place by engaging the landscape.

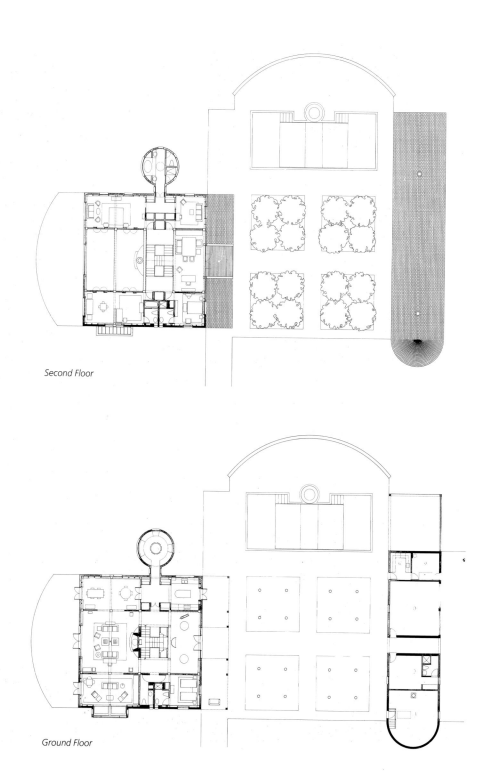

Second Floor

Ground Floor

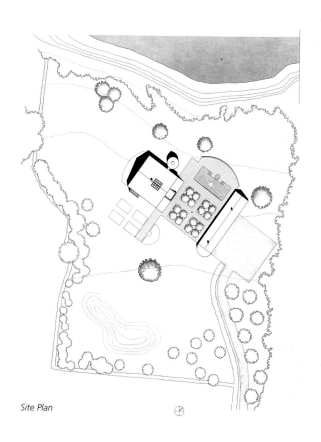

Site Plan

Above: *The floor of the barn and the court-yard are co-planar, reinforcing the idea of the courtyard as the outdoor equivalent of the enclosed barn volume. The front porch is an addition to the original structure; its column bays reflect the interior circulation and frame the sixteen pear trees.*

Bottom Left: *A shade porch frames the view of the pool and the pond beyond.*

Bottom Right: *A single maple tree, on axis with the pool terrace, defines the front lawn.*

Right: The original siding of the barn is revealed on the interior, and the partition walls are "half-timbered" to create the reading of the living room as a town square.

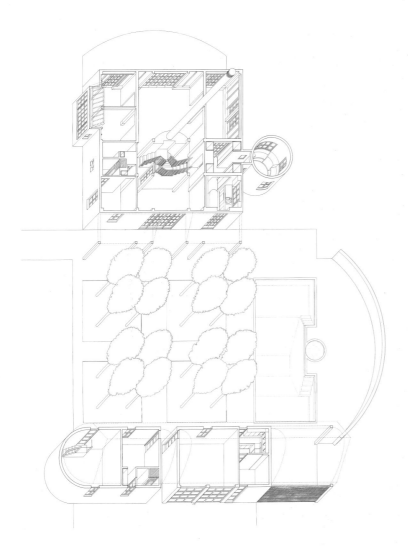

This Page: *The interconnected stair and chimney in the central volume of the barn are clearly rendered not as part of the original structure, but as a new object within a frame.*

The barn's structure divides the house naturally into sixteen square bays. A split staircase, lit by a skylight at the peak of the roof, and a massive, sand-finished stucco fireplace are the primary architectural interventions in the barn's central volume, dominating the low, double-square entry hall to the north and the four-square, two-and-a-half story living room to the south. A twenty-foot high expanse of glass in the south facade recalls the barn's original entrance and leads to a second terrace overlooking the pond and the marsh grass at the southern edge of the site.

On axis with the stair, a silo-shaped pavilion containing the breakfast room on the ground floor, and the master bathroom above, looks out over the pond in three directions. On the second floor, the master bedroom and the child's bedroom and play area face each other across the living room. Their shuttered windows reinforce the outdoor impression of the half-timbered walls and make the living room into a village square, the central meeting place of the house. At the front of the house, a half-level above the bedrooms, a window in the large study reveals, across the pond, a glimpse of the ocean in the distance.

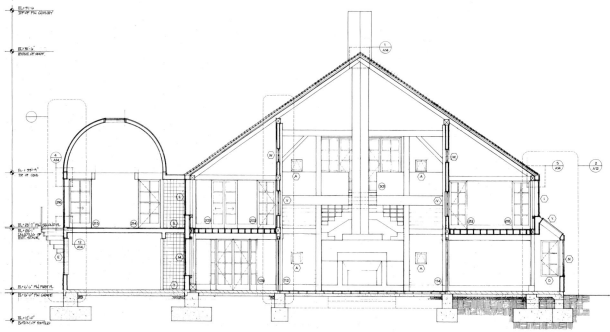

Left: *Brick flooring defines an asymmetrical, west-oriented cross-axis that culminates in the "silo," with 240-degree views of the pond. The furniture, built-in cabinets and a Stickley table with wedge-shaped chairs, is integrated into the architectonics of the circular breakfast room.*

Opel Residence

Shelburne, Vermont

A twelve-acre wooded site within the historic Shelburne Farms estate is the bucolic setting for a year-round vacation home built for three generations of the Opel family. Four distinct volumes—a bunkhouse that sleeps eight children, two guesthouses, and the main house—are distributed along a spine, forming a series of indoor and outdoor rooms facing Lake Champlain and the Adirondacks. The development of the house as a "village street" creates a series of private retreats among generous spaces for family gatherings.

From the autocourt, in a grove of maples at the southern end of the house, a covered arcade leads past the bunkhouse stairs and a poolside terrace. As it continues along the closed wall of the guesthouses and their terraces, the arcade opens up to the woods and tennis court to the east, generating a sense of anticipation as the view of the lake is first denied and then revealed again upon entering each of the houses.

A fireplace in a glass wall is the interior focus of the two-and-a-half story vaulted living room in the main house. Sliding glass doors extend the living space onto a large terrace overlooking the lake. The breakfast room flows out from the kitchen, forming the southern "wall" of this outdoor room and providing a private deck for the master bedroom above. From the entrance hall, stairs lead up a half-level to a skylit painter's studio in the east wing, and then up again to the master bedroom that looks out towards the lake, and in across the living room to a round window on the north wall, high under the curve of the vault.

The two smaller guesthouses are identical and are variations on the formal strategies of the main house. The vaulted, double-height living spaces each include a sitting area by the fireplace and a small dining area. Sleeping lofts above the kitchens extend back to create the roof over the arcade. Windows high on the south walls bring light into the living rooms; glazed doors in the north walls lead to recessed terraces, giving each house a private outdoor space with views of the lake.

Above: An existing grove of maple trees screens the lawn and swimming pool terrace from the public approach to the house.

Opposite Page: The chimney flues and the curved silhouette of the roofs relate the volumes of the building to the scale of the surrounding landscape.

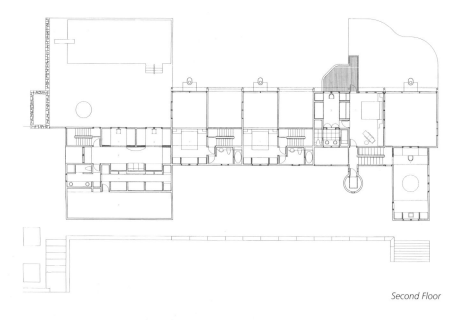

Second Floor

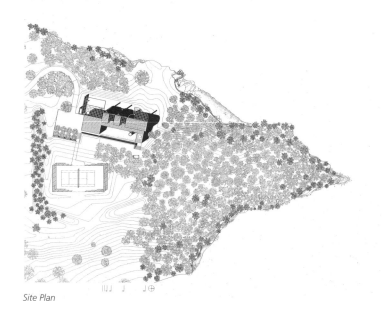

Site Plan

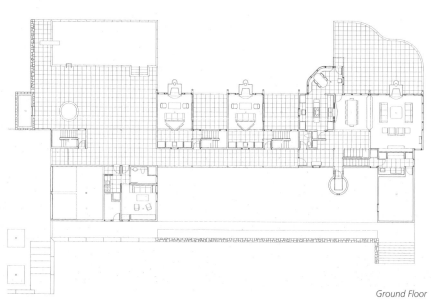

Ground Floor

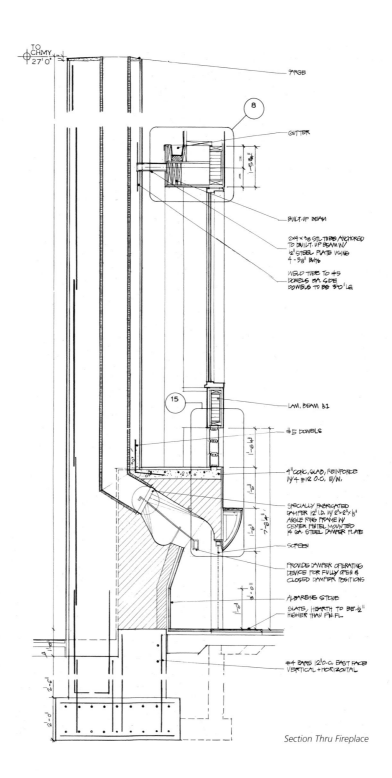

TO
CHMY
27'0"

7ARGE

8

GUTTER

1'-5¾"

BUILT-UP BEAM

2×4 × ⅜ STL TUBE ANCHORED
TO BUILT. UP BEAM W/
½" STEEL PLATE USING
4 - ⅜" BOLTS

WELD TUBE TO #5
DOWELS EA. SIDE
DOWELS TO BE 3'-0" LG.

15

LAM. BEAM B1

#5 DOWELS

1'-6¾"

4" CONC. SLAB. REINFORCE
W/ 4 #12 O.C. E/W.

SPECIALLY FABRICATED
DAMPER 12" I.D. W/ 2"×2"×6"
ANGLE RING FRAME W/
CENTER PINTEL MOUNTED
¼ GA. STEEL DAMPER PLATE

7'-8¾"

SCREEN

PROVIDE DAMPER OPERATING
DEVICE FOR FULLY OPEN &
CLOSED DAMPER POSITIONS

ALBARENE STONE

SLATE HEARTH TO BE ½"
HIGHER THAN FIN. FL.

#4 BARS 12" O.C. EAST FACE
VERTICAL + HORIZONTAL

2'-0"

Section Thru Fireplace

Left: *The frame that supports the gutters defines the outer edge of the pavilion/courtyard sequence. The fireboxes are treated as objects on the facade, providing a counterpoint to the transparent, double-height window walls and the recessed terraces. Their glass block surrounds further the effect of a wall with multiple layers of transparency.*

e'

Prior to the Opel residence, space was treated as a series of opaque and transparent layers within a frame. Here, however, the house is developed as a series of objects on a spine, with a more plastic handling of weight and mass. The curves of the roofs become silhouettes as well as sculptural elements in the building's composition; the malleability and soft reflectiveness of their lead-coated surfaces stand in contrast to the house's vertical cedar siding. The deep, square niches of the guest terraces are counterbalanced by the extruded forms of the main terrace and breakfast room. Three identical stucco fireboxes penetrate the glazed walls of the living rooms, their chimneys rising up as freestanding objects to create a complex and rhythmic juxtaposition of solids and voids.

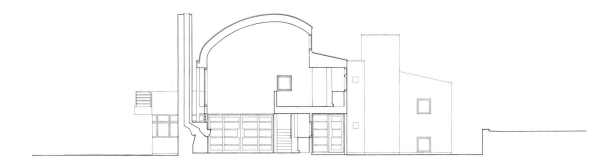

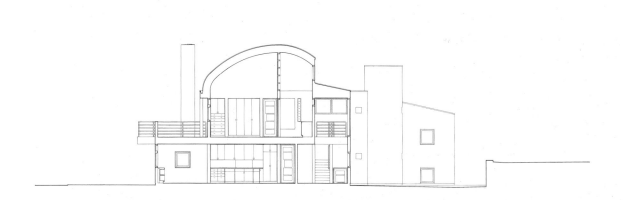

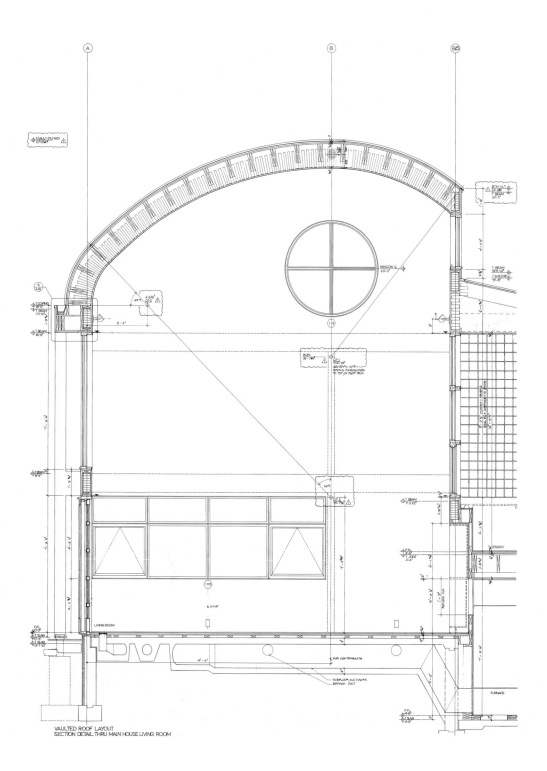

VAULTED ROOF LAYOUT
SECTION DETAIL THRU MAIN HOUSE LIVING ROOM

Left: *The roof vault is a composite curve constructed from three different centerpoints and radii. The modulated shape responds to differing end conditions: the vertical plane of the clerestory window and the horizontal plane of the gutter. The curve extends past the centerline of the circular window, implying closure and creating a complex silhouette rather than a pure geometric segment.*

Steinberg Residence

East Hampton, New York

Set on four acres of dunes on the Atlantic Ocean, the Steinberg residence in East Hampton was built as a week-end retreat and vacation house, with separate caretaker's quarters, a tennis court, and an outdoor swimming pool. The house adapts the parti of the deMenil residence to a sloped terrain, using a natural change in level to create a bridge between the more formally landscaped approach to the house and the dunes and oceanfront beyond.

The driveway is flanked by a double hedge that forms the eastern boundary of the site and by a row of cypress trees that screens the caretaker's house and tennis court to the west. The approach leads south toward a grove of pear trees, through which a glimpse of the ocean is visible, and ends in an autocourt that accesses the garage and service areas located on the ground level of the house. A monumental stair leads up one level to the main entrance, marking the axis to the ocean and dividing the house into two zones. To the east are the public areas: the double-height living room, dining room, kitchen, and breakfast room. To the west is a guest bedroom with a sitting room that opens onto the swimming pool ter-race. The stair continues up to a balcony on the second floor which overlooks both the living room and the panorama of the dunes and the ocean, and forms a bridge between the master bedroom and the children's wing.

A series of indoor and outdoor circulation layers wraps the principal living spaces. On the main floor, the northern circu-lation zone continues along the edge of the living room and ends in a second stair that leads down to the service entrance, up to the master dressing room, and then up again to a widow's walk overlooking the ocean. The southern cir-culation zone opens out under the brise-soleil that frames the south facade of the house, creating a transition between the living room and the lawn. The brise-soleil forms an arcade that leads to the pool terrace to the west and to an out-door stair that circles back down to the pear-tree courtyard to the east.

Opposite Page: The monumental front stair forms a retaining wall for a berm that is inte-gral to the section of the house, mediating both the transition from the public approach to the private ocean views, and the change in level from three stories to two.

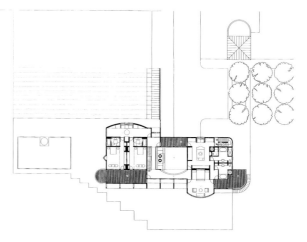

Third Level Plan

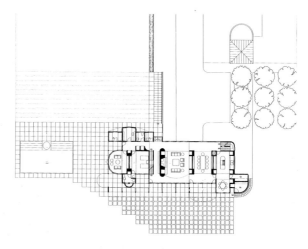

Second Level Plan

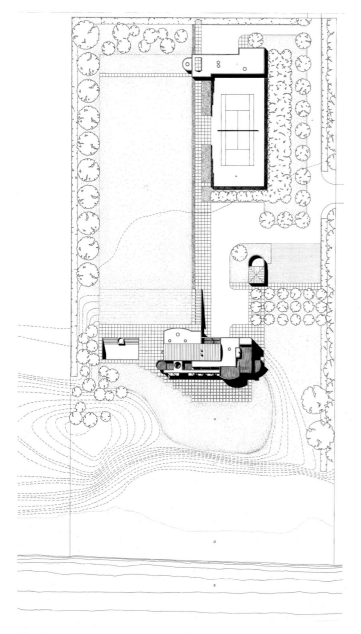

Site Plan

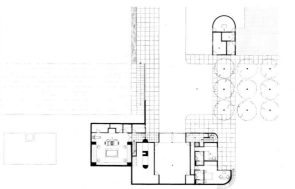

First Level Plan

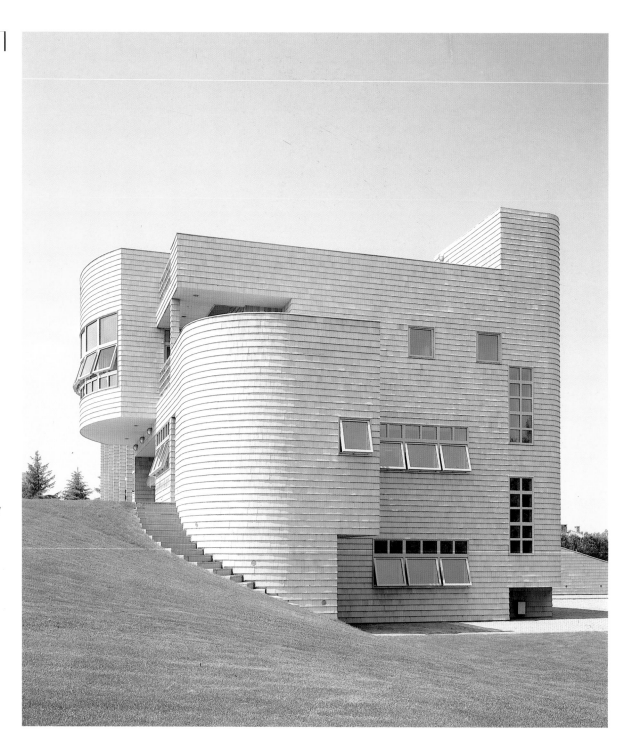

Right: The three-story cast facade is anchored to the landscape by a curved stair/wall that modulates the transition from the autocourt to the ocean front lawn. In contrast, the west façade can be seen as an abstract object "moving" over the landscape.

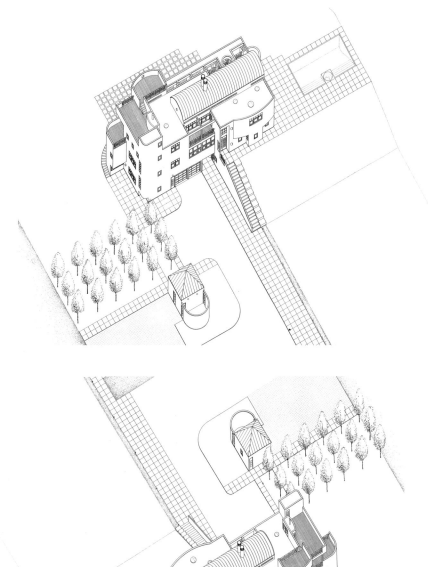

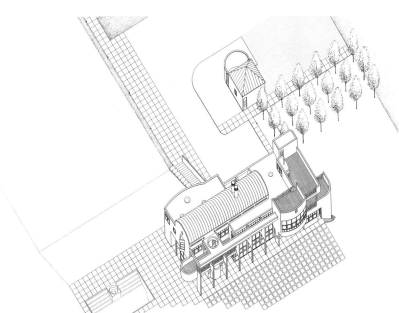

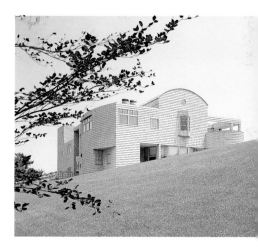

On the second floor, a series of terraces, interrupted by the curved facade of the master bedroom, slides through the brise-soleil. To the west, a deck extends past the children's bedrooms to overlook the swimming pool. To the east, the terrace curves back around the master bedroom, recapturing the view over the pear-tree courtyard and the approach to the house. Coming back around to the north facade, a third terrace overlooks the living room and creates an outdoor link between the children's and parent's sleeping areas.

The curved, lead-coated stainless steel roof marks the central living space and expresses the interior zoning of the house. Differences in orientation and elevation are reflected in the different treatments of the cedar-shingled facades. The three-story north face of the house is a solid plane, punctuated only by a few windows and the long wall of the stair. The two-story southern facade is animated and open, creating a filter between the interior and the landscape that recalls the deMenil house and is a precursor of the Oceanfront residence.

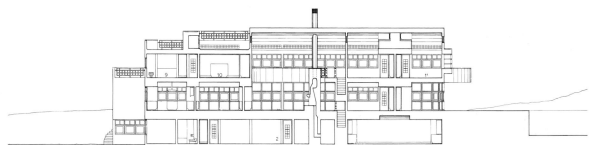

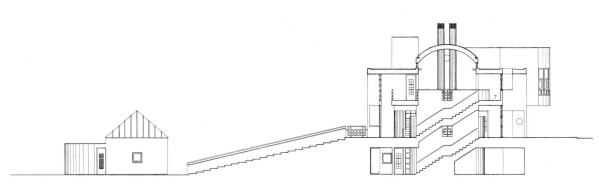

Left: *The barrel-vaulted ceiling extends from the living room through the children's bedrooms to form the profile of the west facade.*

Opposite Page: *In the bedrooms, it is interrupted by a flat soffit that defines a zone that separates the living space from the closets and bathrooms and links the indoor circulation with the decks. The connecting balcony between the children's wing and the master bedroom is curved to extend the volume of the double-height living room and inflect it towards the ocean.*

Oceanfront Residence
California

T he 18,000-square-foot site of the Oceanfront residence is defined to the west by the Pacific Ocean and to the east by the six-lane Pacific Coast Highway. To the north and south, the street is lined by a continuous irregular facade of two-story houses, uninterrupted by street or pedestrian access to the beach. In response to these site conditions, the parti was developed as a combination of typologies. The street facade recalls a rowhouse and is articulated as a series of shallow projections in keeping with the scale of the neighboring buildings. In plan, the building addresses both the urban and natural aspects of the site by eroding a traditional courtyard house and exposing its cut edge to the water, mediating between Southern California's most intensive acoustic and cultural manifestation, the car, and its most serene and peaceful aspect, the ocean.

The entire site is treated as a framework in which pavilions are integrated into a series of open spaces, creating a sequence of layers between the highway and the ocean. The glazed cylinder of the living room becomes the key indoor/outdoor space that interlocks the voids and solids of courtyards and house. The interior is divided into three overlapping zones. The first parallels the street and is occupied by a screening room and guest room on the ground floor and the children's sleeping and play areas above. A service wing on the southern edge of the site contains the garage, kitchen, pantry, and breakfast room on the ground floor, and the staff apartment and master bath and dressing room upstairs. A modest entrance from the street leads between the two wings, through a pear-tree courtyard, to the common family areas overlooking the ocean.

The cylindrical shape of the two-and-a-half story living room recalls the Garey house, but its development responds to the mild California climate rather than the extremes of New England winters and summers. The frame of the cylinder is open in all directions. An eroded arcade to the west modulates the impact of the sun. Beyond the stucco fireplace in the glazed wall, the swimming pool and terrace are visible to the north. To the east, the space flows into a skylit stair

Above: *Responding to the context of the neighborhood, the highway facade is primarily a solid, 150-foot-long wall that defines the frame of the site to the north. Volumetric projections from the plane of the wall relate its scale to nearby buildings.*

Opposite page: *A platform that raises the building above the changing level of the sand becomes the horizontal frame of the site, integrating the pavilions and the outdoor landscaped spaces.*

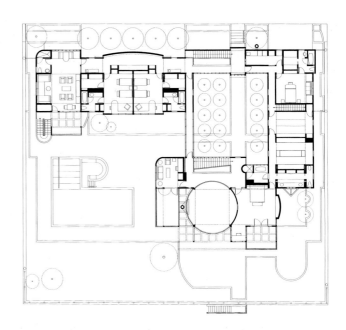

Second Level Plan

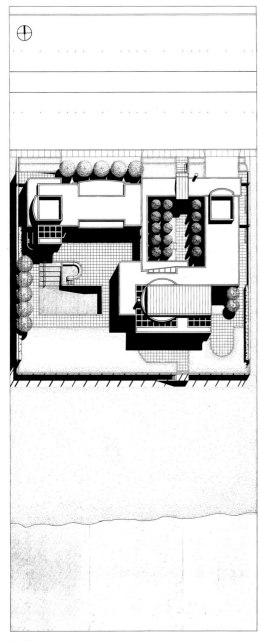

Site Plan

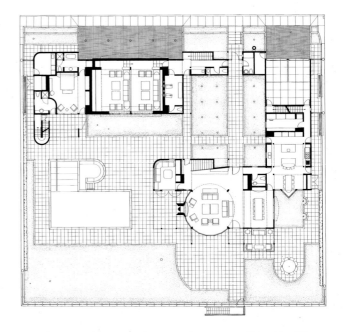

Ground Level Plan

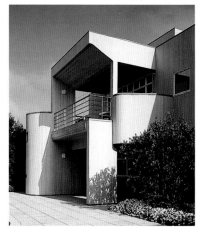

This Page: *Cedar siding is stained a translucent grey, to read uniformly while maintaining the depth and texture of the wood. Wrapped continuously around the surfaces of walls, beams, columns, brise-soleils, and decks, it creates the effect of a plastic material that has been carved from a whole rather than an additive series of elements.*

Right: Steel tubes were placed in the joints between the aluminum mullions to provide structural reinforcement for the glass cylinder. Both fixed and operable windows were given the expression of a split frame.

Opposite Page: French limestone, which remains cool to the touch, even when exposed to the hot sun, was used for both interior and exterior horizontal stone surfaces. Flame-finished pavers define a path through the pear-tree courtyard that intersects the path from the swimming pool terrace.

hall, leading to a balcony on the second floor that looks across the living room to the ocean. To the south, above the dining room, the curved wall of the bedroom is "dematerialized" by the use of pale tiles and a glazed panel that intersects the barrel-vaulted ceiling as it continues back across the master bedroom.

The primary cladding material on the eastern facade is vertical cedar siding. Punctuated only by the entrance, garage door, and a few small windows, its smooth, broadly modulated expanse takes on the appearance of a piece of stone or wood polished by long exposure to the ocean. Aluminum windows dominate the western facade, reinforcing its open, eroded aspect.

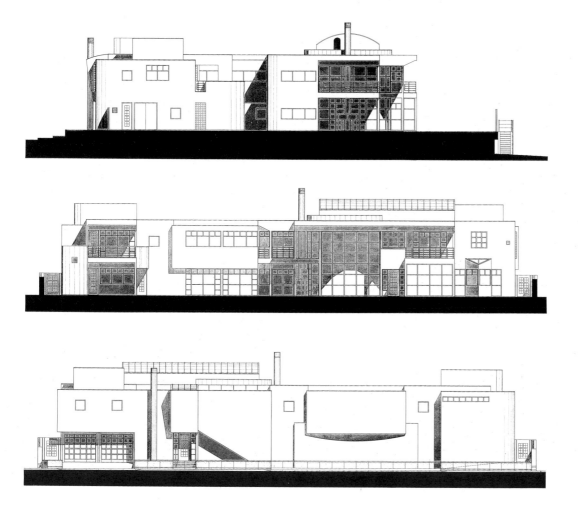

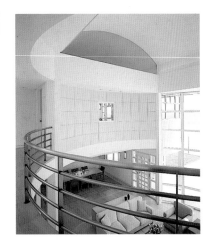

Top: Fabric panels on the curved wall above the dining room conceal audio speakers and soften the acoustics of the main living space. A piece of laminated glass, sixteen feet long and six feet high, maintains the continuity of the barrel-vaulted ceiling between the living room and the master bedroom.

Center and Bottom: At the west end of the balcony, a single row of glass block, inset into the floor, ceiling, and north wall, articulates the intersection of the balcony and the bridge over the courtyard.

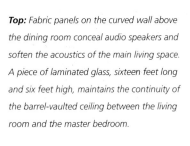

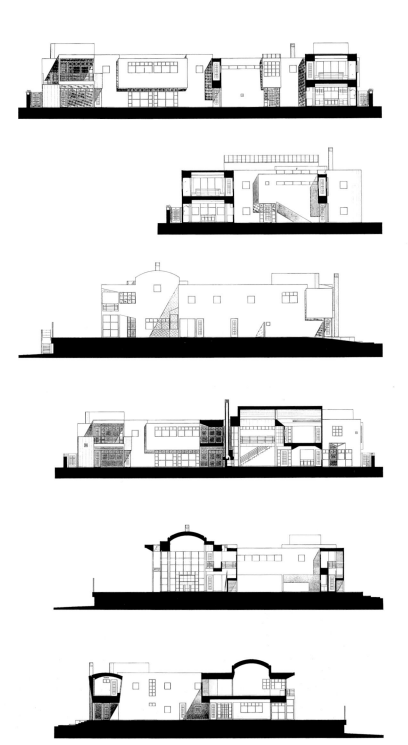

Left: *A wedge-shaped skylight extends the implied volume of the stair vertically. The soffit that modulates the transition between the circular volume of the living room and the edge of the barrel vault steps up to the north, expanding the space above the balcony. .*

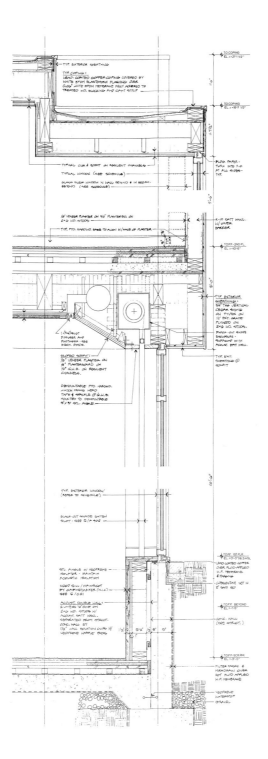

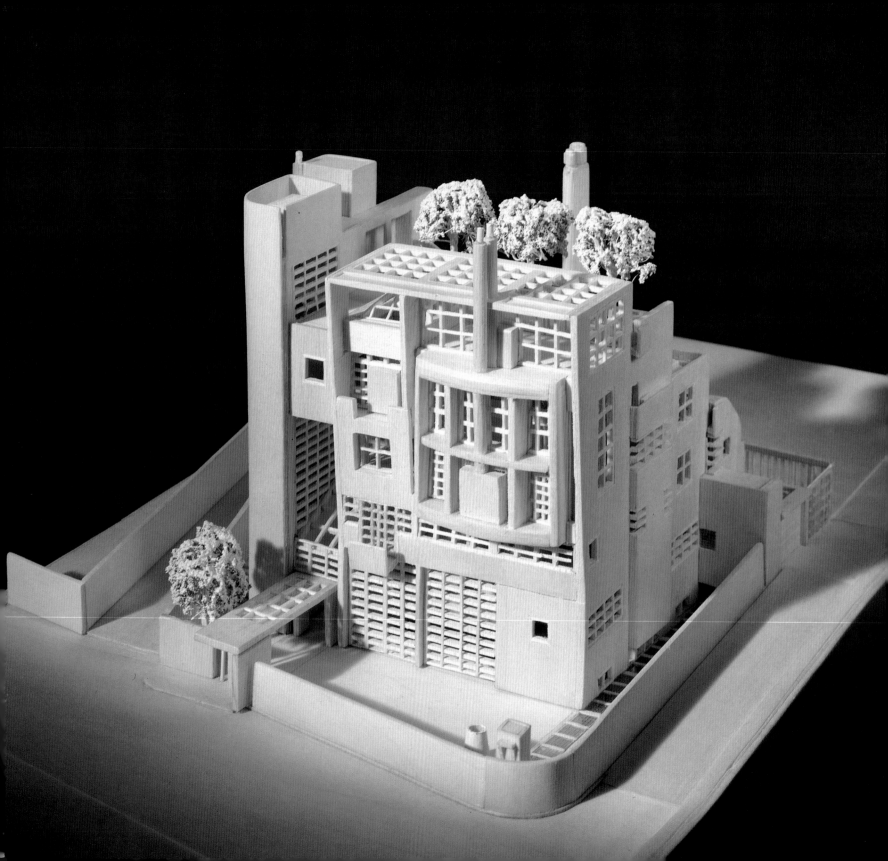

Chen Residence

Taipei, Taiwan

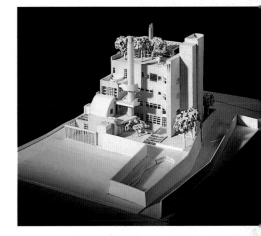

The Chen residence is located in the suburbs of Taipei, on a 10,000 square-foot site with panoramic views of the city's skyline in the distance. Strict zoning regulations limited both the height and the footprint of the building. The owner required extensive facilities for entertaining, but at the same time wanted a house that reflected traditional Chinese values regarding the separation of the public and private spheres of life. Site constraints in combination with the 40,000 square-foot program—three-quarters of which is given over to public entertainment and service spaces—generated a design solution that is straightforward in plan and organization but spatially complex.

The core of the building is a four-and-a-half story atrium/winter garden that visually links the public entertainment areas below grade to the family's gardens and 11,000 square-foot private residence above. A wall of recirculating water creates a vertical indoor reference to the lily pond in the garden. A grand stair under a two-story glass wall leads from the public entrance on the southern edge of the site down to a game room and double-height ballroom and theater. The glass-block floor of the atrium brings natural light into the swimming pool and spa three levels below grade. Service areas, including the staff rooms, mechanical rooms, full-service kitchen, wine cellar, eight-car garage, and car wash, are placed underground around the perimeter of the site.

As though extruded from the gallery, the L-shaped private house extends five stories above grade, becoming an object in the garden. The private entrance provides access to a balcony overlooking the winter garden a half-level above the public entrance, and to a circulation core containing an elevator and stairs. On the second floor, bedrooms for three Chen children and their grandmother look out over the street; a deck, sitting room, and family room look inward to the garden. A formal dining room and double-height living room occupy the street edge of the third floor; the less formal breakfast room, kitchen, and *teppanyaki* room look down on the lily pond. The entire fourth floor is the parents' domain. The master bedroom, lit by a skylight in the roof, overlooks both the living room and the street. A private study,

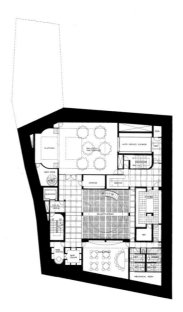

First Basement Plan

Lower Ground Plan

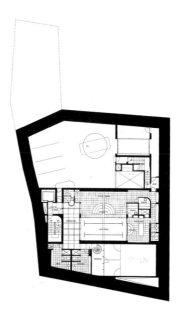

Second Basement Plan

First Basement Mezzanine Plan

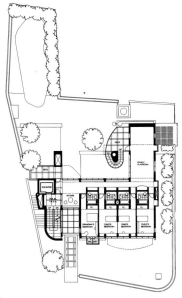

Second Floor Plan

Fourth Floor Plan

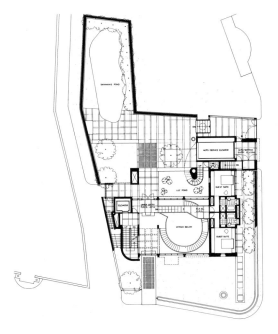

Upper Ground Plan

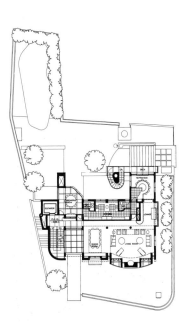

Third Floor Plan

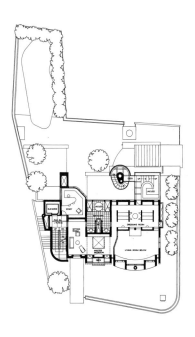

Roof Terrace Plan

bath, dressing room, and outdoor jacuzzi face the garden. On the roof, a screened "moon room" in a garden creates a second ground plane overlooking the panorama of downtown Taipei.

The building is organized sectionally around two helixes. A series of intertwined voids and solids begins in the double-height ballroom, spirals up through the gallery, shifts to the double-height living room, and culminates in the roof garden. A second spiral rotates down around the core of the exterior stair on the garden side of the house, through a series of outdoor terraces and indoor family spaces, coming to rest by the lily pond adjacent to the private entrance. The interweaving of indoor and outdoor creates a natural environment within a dense suburban setting.

The proposed materials of the Chen house were dictated by the labor and technologies available in Taiwan, the high presence of sulphuric acid in Taipei's humid air, and the possibility of earthquakes. Consequently, the frame is reinforced concrete and the primary exterior building materials are granite, stainless steel, and glass, all three of which are self-maintainable and resist the excessive corrosion and mildew caused by the climate.

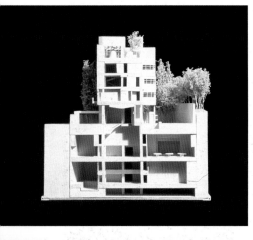

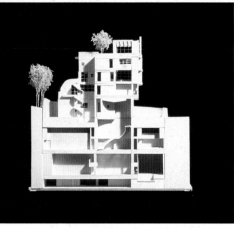

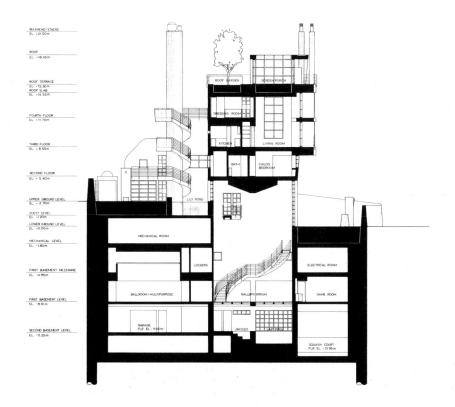

Bechtler Residence

Zumikon, Switzerland

The 27,000-square-foot sloped site of the Bechtler house is located in the town of Zumikon, northeast of Zurich, and affords dramatic views of the Zurichsee and the Alps to the south, and of hillside pastures to the east and north. Swiss zoning laws require that a strict relationship be maintained between the topography of the site and the height of any proposed building, and the parti responds directly to this context. The formal elements of the house are organized as a cluster of interconnected parts whose overlapping fragments evoke images of a rural village that has been built up over time. These planes and volumes are carved into the hillside as a series of terraces, roof terraces, and roof silhouettes, creating a building whose section is literally derived from the slope of the site.

The owners are patrons of the arts who required a separate gallery space to display their significant collection of contemporary painting and sculpture; extensive areas for public entertaining; and privacy for a family of six children. A double-height entry hall provides access from the autocourt to a two-story spine that forms the north-south axis of the house. A line of smooth concrete columns defines the edge of the painting and sculpture gallery on the ground floor and a dining room, which seats 24, above. The other common areas of the house are grouped on the second level, in three distinct volumes at either end of the spine: the kitchen and breakfast room in the south wing; the three-story living room in the north wing; and the library and music room in a glazed cylinder that steps up a quarter-level to overlook the dining area. The living and dining room face a terraced sculpture garden that acts as an outdoor room, complementing the interior public spaces.

A second stair at the north end of the spine extends the full height of the house and accesses the private areas on the third and fourth levels. In the glazed cylinder above the music room, a 180-degree sweep of windows in the master bedroom reveals a panorama of the Alps to the south. A displaced fragment of the cylinder overlooks the living room to the east, forming a private study. The three-level children's "house" is in the northern and uppermost layer of the site, behind

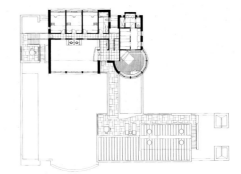

Third Level

Main Level

Site Plan

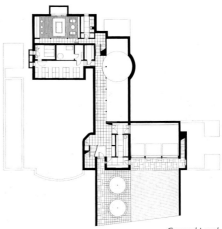

Ground Level

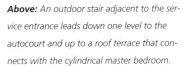

Above: An outdoor stair adjacent to the service entrance leads down one level to the autocourt and up to a roof terrace that connects with the cylindrical master bedroom.

Below: The recessed green limestone wall of the kitchen floats above the garage doors, marking the main entrance from the street. The pattern of the concrete formwork expresses the grid used to organize the house in plan and section, and creates a reveal that conceals the joint between concrete pours.

This Page: *The exterior building materials are divided into three horizontal layers: reinforced concrete at the base, stucco upper walls, and lead-coated standing seam roofs. These elements are juxtaposed as the two- and three-story volumes of the house engage the slope of the hill.*

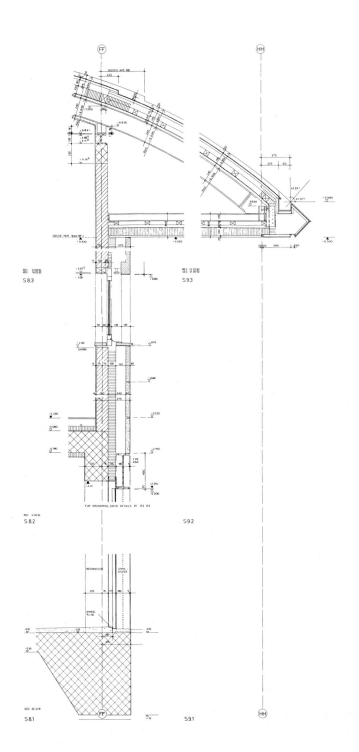

Left: *Expanded metal panels are inset in a stainless steel tubular framework on the interior and exterior handrails, creating a counterpoint between their transparent planes and the dense, material presence of the stone, concrete, and stucco.*

Right: *Custom high-intensity light fixtures between the fireplace flues were designed to illuminate the upper edge of the three-story living room ceiling. Recessed track lights along the reveal in the curve of the plaster ceiling can be directed towards specific artworks, such as Richard Long's mud mural on the end wall.*

the living room. Bedrooms for the girls are a half-level below the parents' bedroom, and overlook the playroom. The boys' rooms are a half-level above, their loft beds tucked high under the curve of the roof. This arrangement affords a sense of privacy and independence while maintaining a feeling of connection between parents' and children's living spaces.

The Zumikon house offered an opportunity to explore the use of cast-in-place concrete, a common regional technology and craft, in a residential context. The dense, physical presence of the concrete reinforces the impression that the house has been carved out of the site. Exterior walls are finished in white stucco and panels of green German limestone, a material that is repeated in the interior in flooring and countertops. The stainless steel of the curved roofs and external stairs is used again in the interior stair details, the dining room ceiling, and the kitchen cabinets and appliances, reinforcing the interplay between indoor and outdoor "rooms."

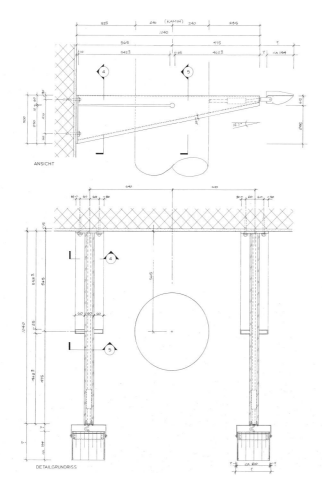

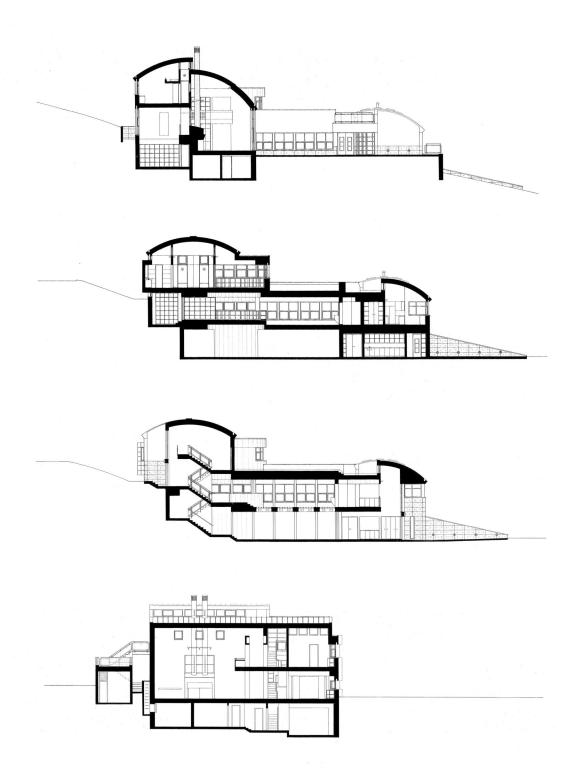

This Page: *The windows in the cylindrical master bedroom and library/music room are rotated 45 degrees off the orthogonal grid of the house to maximize the view of the Alps. The arc of the curved balcony/study that overlooks the living room is determined by the cylinder's centerpoint, revealing a fragment of the whole.*

Hilltop Residence

Austin, Texas

The Hilltop residence is located on a wooded eighty-five acre site overlooking downtown Austin and the University of Texas. The program included an independent entertainment area and extensive on-site parking to accommodate large family gatherings and business functions. Although a separation between parents' and children's private spaces was considered desirable, the owners also wanted the children's indoor and outdoor play spaces visually connected with the adults' living areas.

The building is organized around a horizontal spine, with the "family house" to the northwest and the "entertainment house" to the southeast treated as complex, figural objects within the landscape. The curved roof of the indoor lap pool creates a cross-axial boundary between the two zones. At the top of the hill, a manmade plateau was created by building up the eastern portion of the site to maximize views from the house while preserving existing vegetation. The change in level mediates between the service areas (including a staff apartment, mechanical rooms, and a six-car garage) embedded at grade on the arrival side of the house, and the main floor and a series of outdoor terraces reached by way of the elliptical grand staircase in the skylit entry hall.

The house and topography are integrated to transform the landscape, and passage through the "wall" of the house reveals a series of outdoor "rooms" that reiterate interior programmatic events. At the southeastern corner of the house, a sweep of glazed doors opens from the curved two-story entertainment pavilion onto a series of terraced platforms. These platforms overlook downtown Austin and can be tented to become an outdoor room for large parties and gatherings. The pairing of indoor and outdoor spaces continues around the perimeter of the house in a series of smaller pavilions. A double-height glazed breakfast room extends into an outdoor dining terrace. A corner of the double-height living room is carved away to accommodate a screened sitting porch. The spa, exercise room, and children's playroom are pulled away from the frame of the spine, which opens onto another series of terraces leading down to the outdoor

Opposite page: The axis of the natatorium ends in an organically shaped outdoor swimming pool to the east, and separates the formally landscaped terraces adjacent to the entertainment pavilion from the pool terrace and children's play area to the north.

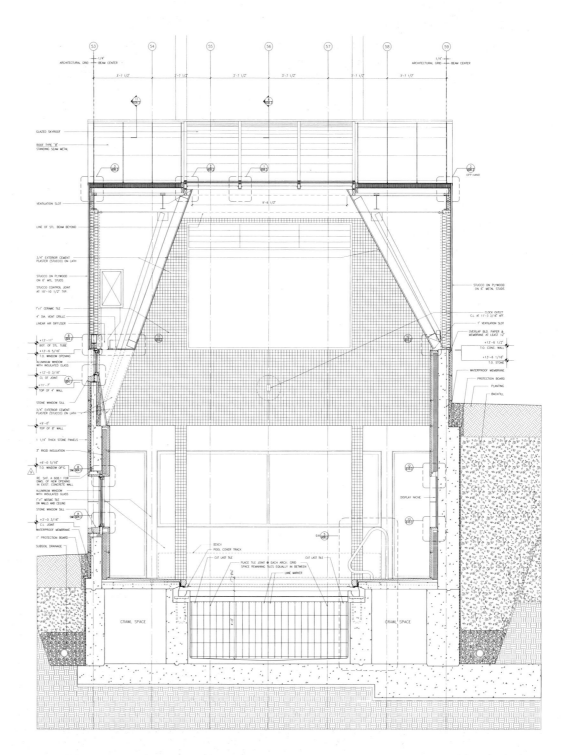

Opposite Page: *A glazed skylight, the same dimensions as the pool, follows the curve of the roof of the natatorium. The plane of the plaster ceiling is curved in two directions. The asymmetrical section responds to the topography of the site. Both sides of the ceiling spring from the top of the retaining wall, which is higher to the south. A horizontal cut reveals a row of windows above the lower northern wall.*

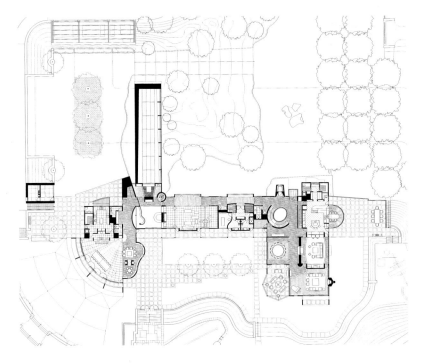

Main Floor Plan

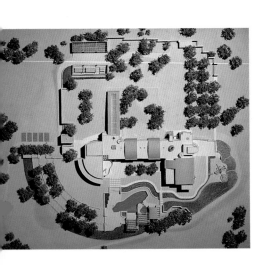

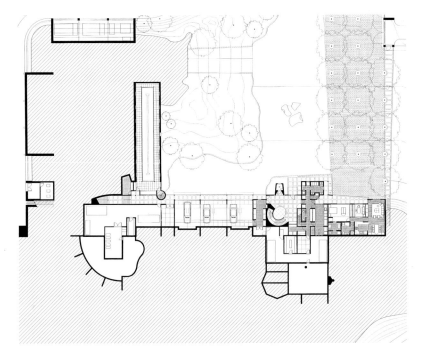

Ground Floor Plan

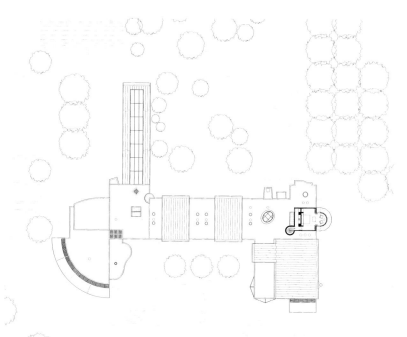

Roof Plan

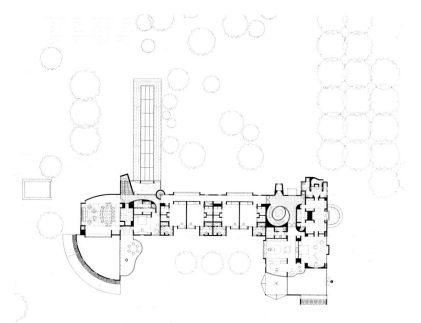

Second Floor Plan

Left: The ground floor plan shows the extent of bermed earth on the eastern and southern slopes of the site. The curved entertainment pavilion, the bedrooms along the spine, and the family pavilion are oriented towards the south-east and views of downtown Austin. Above the roofline, the study in the glazed pavilion captures a view of the lake to the north.

swimming pool, changing rooms, and a bicycle path. The interplay between indoor and outdoor spaces is reinforced in section on the third floor. A guest bedroom and a screening room/conference area in the entertainment zone open to a deck that looks into the double-height entertainment room and out over the pool terrace. The curved study off the master bedroom looks down into the living room, screened porch, and terraces below. The structure of the glazed breakfast room extrudes above the roofline to create a private study for the master bedroom.

Stainless steel wall panels, curved lead-coated stainless steel roofs, and broad expanses of glass articulate the volumes of the pavilions as a series of objects collaged to the stucco frame of the spine. The full extent of the house is visible only from the air. From the ground, it is read as layers of building fragments that are integrated into layers of landscape fragments, and can be comprehended only through memory and speculation as one moves from indoors to outdoors and around the site.

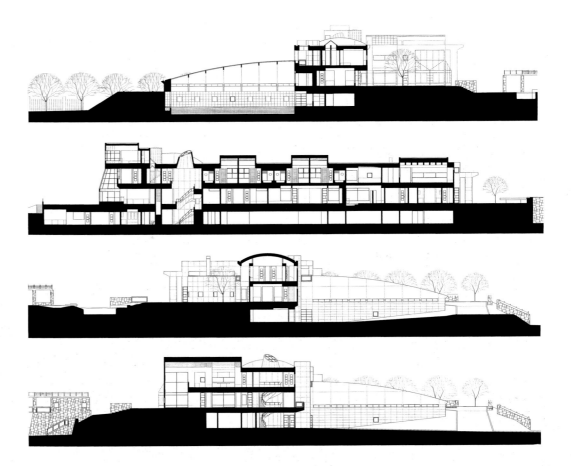

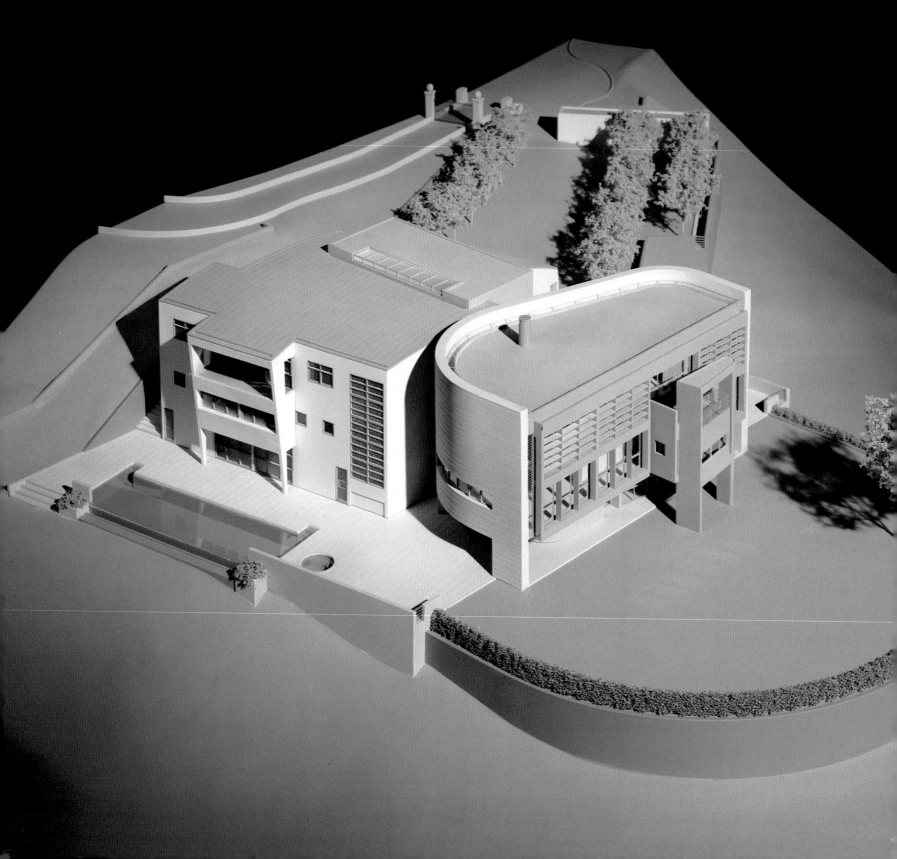

San Onofre Residence
California

T he San Onofre residence is located on one-and-a-half acres in a quiet residential neighborhood near the top of Malibu Canyon. The two-level site suggested a bi-nucleate parti. A three-story curved limestone pavilion, housing the main living spaces, sits on a promontory looking south and east toward Santa Monica, the Pacific Ocean, and the skyline of downtown Los Angeles. A three-story cube containing support space is embedded in the slope behind it, overlooking the canyon to the west.

The support building becomes an object in the land, anchoring and stabilizing the pavilion. The pavilion itself becomes an object on the land, separate, unique, and contrapuntal both in its spatial organization and its rendering. Its curved limestone wall can be read as both a found object and a ruin, transforming the experience of the landscape as one moves through it from the ordered programmatic disposition of the support building into the explosion of space and vistas revealed by the pavilion's glazed facade.

An autocourt at entry level leads from the cul-de-sac to an entrance hall that accommodates the vertical circulation. From it, one passes over a bridge, through the wall of the pavilion, and into the double-height living room. Ahead, the panorama of Santa Monica is silhouetted against the ocean and framed by the stainless steel brise-soleil of the south facade. To the west, a window punched into the curve of the pavilion reveals the prospect of the canyon.

The kitchen and the master bedroom above become an object that floats within the space of the pavilion, forming a boundary between the living room and the formal dining area, with its view towards the skyscrapers of downtown Los Angeles. The breakfast room penetrates the screen of the glazed facade and creates an outdoor terrace for the bedroom above. At ground level, the entertainment room becomes a kind of giant "piloti," recessed within the curve of the pavilion to create a shaded terrace that opens onto the southern lawn and leads back to the swimming pool and spa facing the canyon.

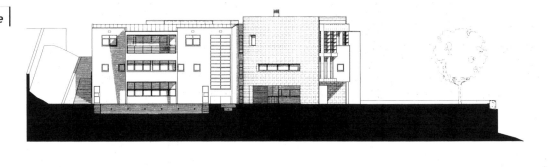

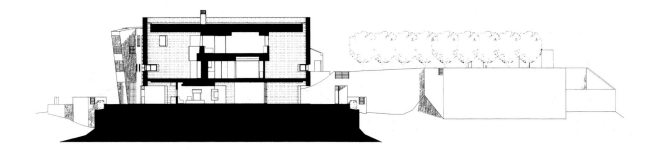

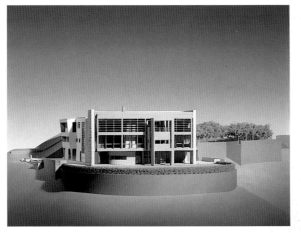

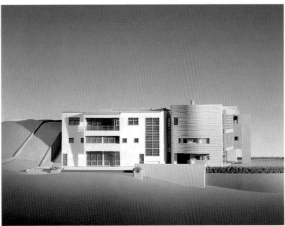

This Page: *The two-foot thick cleft-cut Indiana limestone wall of the pavilion contrasts with the smooth white stucco support building, its rugged texture suggesting a ruin. In the roof, a slot of light separates the wall of the pavilion from the interior, preserving the wall as an independent object.*

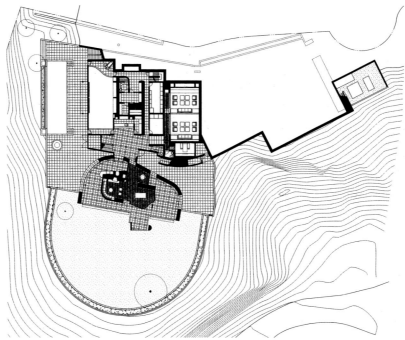

Ground Level Plan

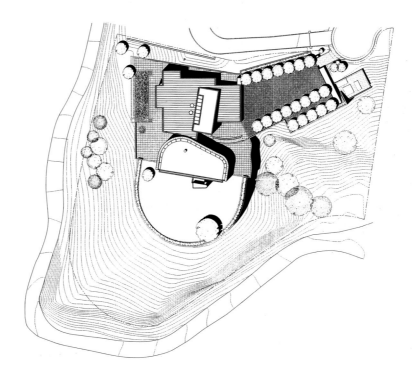

Site Plan

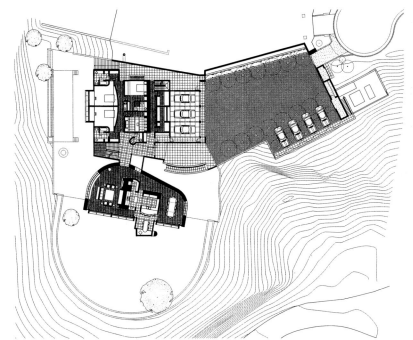

Third Level Plan

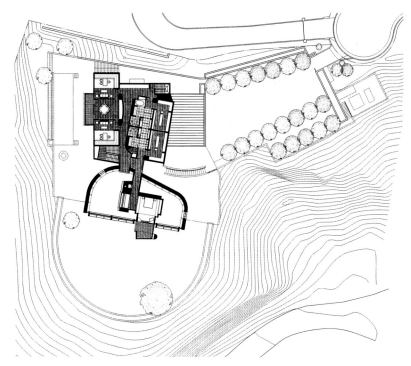

Entry Level Plan

The support building is organized bilaterally. In the light-filled perimeter that looks out over Malibu Canyon are the exercise room on the ground level, the guest bedrooms at entry level, and an office/conference area above on the master bedroom level. In the core, a screening room and archival storage occupy the ground level; storage and service areas are behind the garage on entry level. On the third level, the master dressing room and bath opposite the office are rotated on axis with the bridge that returns to the pavilion.

Seen from above, the juxtapositions of shapes and textures—the cobblestone of the autocourt; the curved pavilion; the objects of the office and master bath floating above the curved zinc-coated roof of the embedded cube—create a cubist bas-relief that is both an abstract composition and a reflection of the internal divisions of private and public spaces. This collage of materials is reiterated in the stainless steel wall panels that articulate the facade of the stuccoed support building and in the stainless steel brise-soleil that contrasts with the curved limestone wall of the pavilion.

The San Onofre residence employs many familiar strategies: the object in the landscape of the Opel and Chen residences; the embedding of the building in the site seen in the Bechtler house; the collaged elements of the Texas house. However, their use here reflects a less analytic, more poetic and intuitive response to a site that offered unique contrasts between the urban, the manmade, and the natural, as well as variations in scale ranging from the immediacy of the canyon terrain to the immensity of the ocean's horizon.

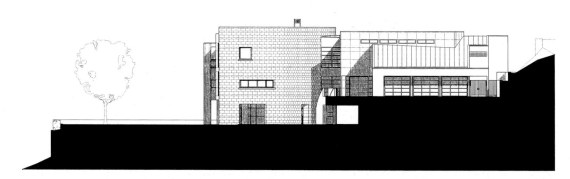

Selected Buildings and Projects

Steinberg Residence
East Hampton, New York

Project Staff: Gustav Rosenlof,
Associate, Joan Jasper, Malka van
Bemmelen, Joan Pierpoline
Site: 4 acres
Building: 8,500 sf
Date of design: 1986
Date construction completed: 1989

Bechtler Residence
Zumikon, Switzerland

Project Staff: Bruce Donnally,
Associate, Nancy Clayton, Thomas
Lewis, Sylvia Becker;
Associate Architect: Pfister & Schiess
Architekten
Site: 26,900 sf (2,500 sm)
Building: 10,225 sf (950 sm)
Date of design: 1990
Date construction completed: 1994

deMenil Residence
East Hampton, New York

Project Staff: Bruce Nagel, Associate,
Paul Aferiat, Henry Ayon, Frank Lupo,
Barry McCormick, John Meder, Thomas
Phifer, Daniel Rowen, David Steinman
Site: 6 acres
Building: 10,000 sf
Date of design: 1979
Date construction completed: 1983

Spielberg Residence
East Hampton, New York

Project Staff: Jose Coriano, Associate,
Kerry Moran
Site: 6 acres
Building: 5,000 sf
Date of design: 1985
Date construction completed: 1988

Oceanfront Residence
California

Project Staff: Gerald Gendreau,
Associate, Anthony Iovino, Nancy
Clayton, Gregory Epstein,
Paul Mitchell
Site: 18,000 sf
Building: 11,000 sf
Date of design: 1988
Date construction completed: 1993

Hilltop Residence
Austin, Texas

Project Staff: Gustav Rosenlof,
Associate, Juan Miró, Meta
Brunzema, Frank Thaler,
Richard Lucas
Site: 85 acres
Building: 28,000 sf
Date of design: 1993
Under construction

Garey Residence
Kent, Connecticut

Project Staff: Jose Coriano, Associate,
Frank Lupo
Site: 9 acres
Building: 4,000 sf
Date of design: 1983
Date construction completed: 1988

Opel Residence
Shelburne, Vermont

Project Staff: Paul Aferiat, Associate,
Reynolds Logan
Site: 12 acres
Building: 7,000 sf
Date of design: 1985
Date construction completed: 1987

Chen Residence
Taipei, Taiwan

Project Staff: Jacob Alspector,
Associate, Gregory Karn,
Gregory Epstein, Tsun-Kin Tam
Site: 10,000 sf
Building: 40,000 sf
Date of design: 1990
(project)

San Onofre Residence
California

Project Staff: Gerald Gendreau,
Associate, Greg Epstein, Joseph Hsu,
Peter Pawlak
Site: 1.5 acres
Building: 18,000 sf
Date of design: 1993
Under construction

Firm Profile

Gwathmey Siegel & Associates Architects is one of the country's most acclaimed and honored architectural firms. Since its inception in 1967, its work has ranged in scale from distinguished arts and educational facilities and major corporate buildings to furniture systems and decorative art objects. In 1994 the office won an international competition to design the Nanyang Polytechnic in Singapore, a 75-acre, 2.3 million-square-foot comprehensive university campus. Among its many notable recent achievements are the Contemporary Resort Convention Center at Walt Disney World; the Solomon Equities office building in New York; the School of Agriculture, the Fieldhouse and Basketball Arena, and the Theory Center at the College of Engineering at Cornell University; Werner Otto Hall, The Busch Reisinger Museum, and Fine Arts Library addition to the Fogg Museum at Harvard University; and the restoration and addition to Frank Lloyd Wright's Solomon R. Guggenheim Museum in New York. Projects under construction include the Henry Art Museum, University of Washington, Seattle; the Social Sciences Building at the University of California at San Diego; and the Science, Industry and Business Library of the New York Public Library.

In 1982 Gwathmey Siegel & Associates Architects became the youngest firm ever to be awarded the American Institute of Architects' highest honor — the Firm Award — for "approaching every project with a fresh eye, a meticulous attention to detail, a keen appreciation for environmental and economic concerns, an unswerving dedication to design excellence, and a strong belief in collaborative effort." Both Charles Gwathmey and Robert Siegel are Fellows of the American Institute of Architects and recipients of the Medal of Honor from its New York Chapter.

Residential work continues to be a foundation of Gwathmey Siegel's investigations. Since the design of the Gwathmey Residence and Studio in Amagansett in 1964, the building of houses has been seen as an important laboratory for the exploration of architectural strategies. This volume examines developments in the firm's work over the past sixteen years, and features the deMenil, Spielberg, and Bechtler residences, as well as designs for houses in California, New England, Texas, and Taiwan.

bove: *Charles Gwathmey and Robert Siegel*

Photographic Credits